Pebble® Plus
Bilingüe/Bilingual

¿QUÉ HAY EN MiPlato?

PROTEÍNAS en MiPlato

WHAT'S ON MyPlate?

PROTEIN on MyPlate

por/by Mari Schuh

Editora consultora/Consulting Editor:
Gail Saunders-Smith, PhD

Consultora/Consultant: Barbara J. Rolls, PhD
Guthrie Chair en Nutrición/Guthrie Chair in Nutrition
Pennsylvania State University
University Park, Pennsylvania

CAPSTONE PRESS
a capstone imprint

Pebble Plus is published by Capstone Press,
1710 Roe Crest Drive, North Mankato, Minnesota 56003
www.capstonepub.com

Library of Congress Cataloging-in-Publication Data
Schuh, Mari C., 1975–
 [Protein on my plate. Spanish & English]
 Proteínas en miplato = Protein on myplate / por Mari Schuh ; editora consultora, Gail Saunders-Smith.
  p. cm.—(Pebble Plus bilingue. ¿Qué hay en miplato? = Pebble Plus bilingual. What's on myplate?)
 In English and Spanish.
 Audience: K to grade 3.
 Includes index.
 ISBN 978-1-62065-945-8 (library binding)
 ISBN 978-1-4765-1765-0 (ebook PDF)
 1. Proteins in human nutrition—Juvenile literature. 2. Food—Protein content—Juvenile literature. I. Title. II. Title:
Protein on myplate.
 TX553.P7S3818 2013
 613.2'82—dc23   2012022674

Summary: Simple text and photos describe USDA's MyPlate tool and healthy protein choices
for children—in both English and Spanish

Editorial Credits
Jeni Wittrock, editor; Strictly Spanish, translation services; Eric Manske, bilingual book designer; Sarah Bennett,
designer; Svetlana Zhurkin, media researcher; Jennifer Walker, production specialist; Sarah Schuette, photo stylist;
Marcy Morin, studio scheduler

Photo Credits
All photos by Capstone Studio/Karon Dubke except:
Shutterstock: BW Folsom, cover (bottom left), Igor Klimov, cover (top right), Pshenichka, cover (bottom right), Tristan
Tan, back cover; USDA, cover (inset), 5

The author dedicates this book to Devon Borst of Pleasant Prairie, Wisconsin,
who makes the best hard-boiled eggs in southeastern Wisconsin.

Information in this book supports
the U.S. Department of Agriculture's
MyPlate food guidance system found at
www.choosemyplate.gov. Food amounts
listed in this book are based on daily
recommendations for children ages 4-8.
The amounts listed in this book are
appropriate for children who get less than
30 minutes a day of moderate physical
activity, beyond normal daily activities.
Children who are more physically active
may be able to eat more while staying
within calorie needs. The U.S. Department
of Agriculture (USDA) does not endorse
any products, services, or organizations.

Note to Parents and Teachers

The ¿Qué hay en MiPlato?/What's on MyPlate? series supports national science standards
related to health and nutrition. This book describes and illustrates the USDA's recommendations
on protein. The images support early readers in understanding the text. The repetition of words
and phrases helps early readers learn new words. This book also introduces early readers to
subject-specific vocabulary words, which are defined in the Glossary section. Early readers may
need assistance to read some words and to use the Table of Contents, Glossary, Internet Sites,
and Index sections of the book.

Printed in China.
092012   006934LEOS13

Table of Contents

Tabla de contenidos

MyPlate/ MiPlato

Protein foods are an important part of MyPlate. MyPlate is a tool that helps you choose healthful food.

Las proteínas son una parte importante de MiPlato. MiPlato es una herramienta que te ayuda a comer alimentos saludables.

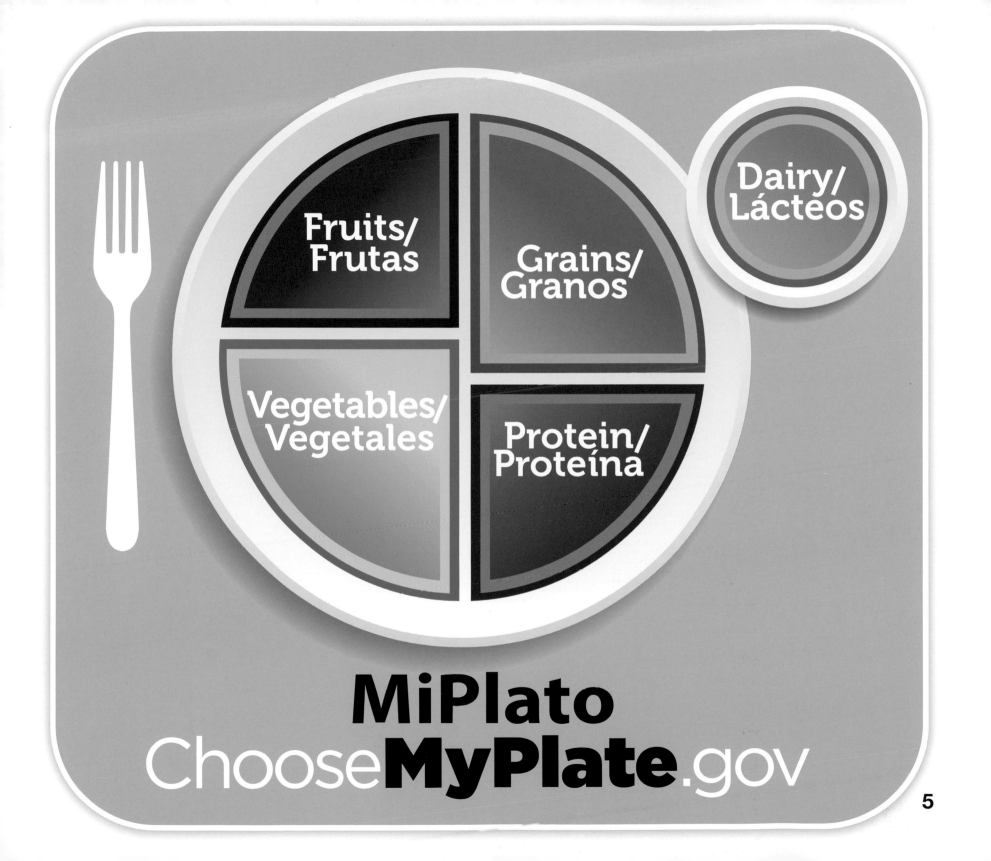

MiPlato
ChooseMyPlate.gov

5

Protein/ Proteínas

Meats like chicken, beef,
and fish are protein foods.
Beans, eggs, nuts, and seeds
are also full of protein.

Las carnes como pollo, res y pescado
son alimentos con proteínas.
Los frijoles, los huevos, las nueces y las
semillas también están llenos de proteínas.

Protein helps build
bones and muscles.
Protein-rich foods
are full of nutrients.

Las proteínas ayudan a formar
huesos y músculos.
Los alimentos ricos en proteínas
están llenos de nutrientes.

Every day, eat 4 ounces

(110 grams) of protein.

Try to eat different

protein foods every week.

Cada día, come 4 onzas

(110 gramos) de proteínas.

Trata de comer diferentes alimentos

con proteínas cada semana.

11

Eat lean protein.

Lean protein is low in fat.

Have an adult trim away the fat
from meat before cooking.

Come proteínas magras.

La proteína magra es baja en grasas.

Deja que un adulto corte toda la grasa
de la carne antes de cocinarla.

Enjoying Protein Foods/ Disfrutar alimentos con proteínas

Good morning!

Start the day with protein.

Eat ham and eggs for breakfast.

¡Buenos días!

Empieza el día con proteínas.

Come jamón con huevos para el desayuno.

14

15

Mixed nuts make

a crunchy snack.

Sprinkle nuts on frozen yogurt.

La mezcla de nueces es

una merienda crocante.

Rocía nueces sobre yogur congelado.

It's lunchtime.

Make a sandwich.

Choose peanut butter, tuna,
sliced lean meat, or a veggie burger.

Es hora de almorzar.

Prepara un sándwich.

Selecciona mantequilla de maní, atún, rebanadas
de carne magra o una hamburguesa vegetariana.

How Much to Eat/ Cuánto comer

Many kids need to eat about 4 ounces (110 grams) of protein every day. To get 4 ounces, pick four servings of your favorite food.

Muchos niños necesitan comer alrededor de 4 onzas (110 gramos) de proteína cada día. Para obtener 4 onzas, selecciona cuatro porciones de tus alimentos favoritos.

1 tablespoon (15 mL) peanut butter

1 cucharada (15 ml) de mantequilla de maní

¼ cup (60 mL) refried beans

¼ taza (60 ml) de frijoles refritos

1 egg

1 huevo

½ ounce (15 grams) sunflower seeds

½ onza (15 gramos) de semillas de girasol

1 ounce (30 grams) tuna

1 onza (30 gramos) de atún

2 tablespoons (30 mL) hummus

2 cucharadas (30 ml) de hummus

1 slice lean turkey

1 rebanada de pavo magro

½ veggie burger

½ hamburguesa vegetariana

Glossary

muscle—a tissue in the body that is made of strong fibers; muscles can be tightened or relaxed to make the body move

Myplate—a food plan that reminds people to eat healthful food and be active; MyPlate was created by the U.S. Department of Agriculture

nutrient—something that people need to eat to stay healthy and strong; vitamins and minerals are nutrients

protein—a substance found in plant and animal cells; your body needs protein to stay healthy

veggie burger—a burger made from vegetables, soybeans, and nuts; veggie burgers do not have any meat in them

Internet Sites

FactHound offers a safe, fun way to find Internet sites related to this book. All of the sites on FactHound have been researched by our staff.

Here's all you do:

Visit *www.facthound.com*

Type in this code: 978162069458

Check out projects, games and lots more at
www.capstonekids.com

Glosario

la hamburguesa vegetariana—una hamburguesa hecha con vegetales, frijoles de soja y nueces; las hamburguesas vegetarianas no tienen carne

MiPlato—un plan de alimentos que hace recordar a la gente de comer alimentos saludables y de estar activos; MiPlato fue creado por el Departamento de Agricultura de EE.UU.

el músculo—un tejido del cuerpo que está formado por fibras fuertes; los músculos pueden ser contraídos o relajados para mover al cuerpo

el nutriente—algo que la gente necesita comer para permanecer saludable y fuerte; las vitaminas y los minerales son nutrientes

la proteína—una sustancia en células de plantas y animales; tu cuerpo necesita proteínas para permanecer saludable

Sitios de Internet

FactHound brinda una forma segura y divertida de encontrar sitios de Internet relacionados con este libro. Todos los sitios en FactHound han sido investigados por nuestro personal.

Esto es todo lo que tienes que hacer:

Visita: *www.facthound.com*

Ingresa este código: 978162069458

Index

Índice